LOVE *the* EVERYDAY
The Art of Joyful Living

Know God's Goodness Each Day

Written & Illustrated by Sarah Graham

To Tommy, thank you for the joy of loving you *every day*.

a little note to you

Welcome to this little book about the art of joyful living. Before we dive in, I wanted to give you 3 simple tips to help you yield the most out of these pages.

step 1

Download your free copy of the *Love the Everyday Workbook* on my website.
Go to—humblydesigned.com/workbookgift

step 2

Use the note pages at the end of each chapter to write your thoughts and reflections.

step 3

Colour me in! This book is designed for you to colour in and make it your own. And if you do, I'd love for you to share a photo with me over on Instagram—@humblydesigned.

Love the Everyday: The Art of Joyful Living

Copyright © 2025 by Sarah Graham

ISBN: 978-1-7636623-0-8

Written and illustrated by Sarah Graham

Bible translation referenced—New International Version

All rights reserved. No part of this publication may be reproduced, distributed, or transmitted in any form or by any means, including photocopying, recording, or other electronic or mechanical methods, without the prior written permission of the publisher, except in the case of brief quotations embodied in critical reviews and certain other noncommercial uses permitted by copyright law.

contents

introduction	9
slowing	15
habits	29
interruption	39
gratitude	47
savour	57
senses	69
seasons	83
outdoors	97
movement	109
play	121
creativity	129
order	141
simplicity	147
home	155
nourish	161
work	167
gather	173
giving	185

introduction

Every good and perfect gift is from above, coming down from the Father of the heavenly lights, who does not change like shifting shadows. — James 1:17

What brings you joy? Perhaps the waking moment when you swing open the curtains as you feel the sun's golden warmth on your squinting face, or getting swept up in a bubbling conversation with a counterpart who exuberantly shares your passion for crocheting hats.

During the summer of 2020, I stumbled upon a transformative practice that changed the way I perceived the world. It started with a humble list – a catalogue of the simple delights I encountered in the course of my everyday life. At first, it was merely a bit of fun, a bit of whimsy to brighten my routine. Little did I know that this seemingly trivial endeavour would evolve into a profound way of living. A way of living that would help combat discontentment, remind me of what was important and foster a deeper love for the everyday.

Life is full of goodness and beauty. And the way we interact with the mundanity of life, the repetition, the ordinary moments, hugely shapes our minds, our lives—the very person we become.

Have you ever noticed how two people can be doing an activity simultaneously while one is brimming with joy and the other not. A joy filled life is often more about our attitude toward the present moment than the circumstances we're in.

I hear you, not all of life is roses and sunshine. There are seasons when life is painful, challenging, overwhelming. However, often these times can grow us and open us up to an even deeper appreciation toward what we do have. Loving the everyday isn't about staying positive or maximising pleasure, but rather about learning to be present in the wonderful and hard moments of life while continually embracing the goodness that each day has—offering us a sort of balance to the melange of life. I've found there to be such a richness when we open our eyes to God's goodness and glory in all seasons.

I think of my sweet Grandma who had such a deep love of nature. Most mornings she would sit outside in the soft golden sun, drinking her tea and murmuring prayers. She liked to call herself a solar panel, jovially stating, 'I get my energy from the sun!' In her frailty, Ma was no longer able to go out alone. One glorious sunny day she said to me, 'Sarah it is the most beautiful day, so I asked the Lord to make a way for me to go to the beach.' As she was telling me this, she had just gotten off the phone with her dear friend who had invited to pick her up and take her to the beach. Ma was chuffed, ecstatic! 'Praise the Lord,' she sang, with great enthusiasm. Ma's love for nature and intimate relationship with her heavenly Father were so intertwined and evident to see. This story reminds me of God's heart for us. He desires to give us good gifts, and He wants us to ask for them. As Mathew 7:11 states, 'If you, then, though you are evil, know how to give good gifts to your children, how much more will your Father in heaven give good gifts to those who ask him!' Do you believe God wants to bless you in your everyday life?

My hope is that these pages help to reframe your mind to appreciate what you have as gifts. Gifts to be received with gratitude and held loosely as you look for ways to generously share them with those around you.

These pages are filled with a plethora of ideas and inspiration that you may wish to implement into your life. However these ideas are designed to be gentle suggestions and invitations, rather than must do actions. Please don't feel pressured to make grandiose changes, or try anything that isn't aligned with your season of life. You may even enjoy reading one chapter at a time and thoughtfully contemplate each topic slowly and intentionally. You'll also notice how a couple of ideas and prompts are repeated in different chapters as they relate to numerous areas.

I also invite you to download the free *Love the Everyday Workbook* to get access to a bundle of thoughtfully curated activity pages that align with each chapter of the book. Head to *humblydesigned.com/workbookgift* to download and print your gift.

This book offers practical and actionable ways to help you rediscover the beauty hidden within the ordinary moments of your day. So as you read this, I invite you to grab that cute mug you have a deep emotional attachment to, pour a comforting warm drink, curl up in your cosiest spot and join me on this journey of joy. Whether you're seeking to cultivate gratitude, ignite your creativity, or simply be reminded of God's goodness in each day, this book has you covered.

slowing

He says, 'Be still, and know that I am God; I will be exalted among the nations I will be exalted in the earth.'
— Psalm 46:10

Slowness is a friend of joy. Yes, joy can be found in the celebration of loved ones and the rush of a rollercoaster. However, there is another type of joy. One that is shy, revealing itself only in the unhurried, quiet and gentle moments, otherwise unnoticed in the whirlwind of haste. This joy is rich, yet somewhat delicate. It requires our attention and our willingness to be present.

One chilled winter's day, I trekked up a grassy English moor alone, cheerfully unaware of my numb legs that would later give me frost bite. The whole adventure was delightful. However, halfway down, I passed a wooden bench and decided to take a seat. As I blithely gazed over the lavish rolling hills of the enchanting countryside, I felt my body and mind slowing to the peaceful pace of my surroundings. I felt such a profound sense of stillness and unhurried joy. To this day, that simple moment of slowness is one of my most cherished memories. Yet what astounds me most, is how easily I could have ignored that little bench in the endeavour to finish my quest. And in many ways I do in my daily life. It's so easy to turn a blind eye to little opportunities of slowness and mindfulness throughout our days. We go from one thing to the next, filling our lives with activities, to-do lists and entertainment. However, there is such a joy to be found when you intentionally grasp little moments of pause, rest and slowness each day. For me this often looks like taking a sip of my freshly brewed tea with slowness and delightful care, or choosing to pause and take a deep, refreshing breath before moving to my next task. What small moments of slowness do you enjoy?

Slow living will mean many different things to different people. You might associate a slow life with a homestead in the countryside, or living in a vintage shack by the beach. Yet for me, I live in an apartment in the city, where rush and noise is ample. And although this can cause friction to living slowly, I love to seek out simple ways to slow down and find joy in unhurried moments.

Many of us live busy lives, and the idea of living slowly may sound impractical or unobtainable. However as we realign our priorities, rest well and give ourselves margin, slowing down can actually help reduce time wasting activities and give us more time for what truly matters.

I love this quote from John Mark Comer's book *The Ruthless Elimination of Hurry*. 'To walk with Jesus is to walk with a slow, unhurried pace. Hurry is the death of prayer and only impedes and spoils our work. It never advances it.'

I invite you, right now, to take a deep breath, pause, look around you. What beauty do you see? Sink it in and enjoy it.

slow daily rhythms

Here is a list of daily rhythms to inspire a gentle, intentional and slower way of life.

walk leisurely through nature

start and end the day with no technology

soak up the morning sun

spend time on a mindful hobby

savour making and drinking your morning tea or coffee

take 5 minutes to be still and silent

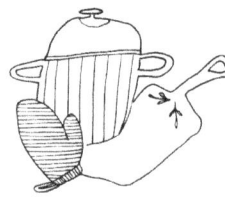
cook a delicious meal from scratch

journal

carve out a specific time for prayer and mindfulness

slow weekly rhythms

Weekly rhythms are a wonderful opportunity to reset, reconnect and reflect. I hope these ideas inspire you to carve out time for what is most important to you each week.

go on an adventure through nature

spend a while in silence and solitude

catch up with a loved one and linger

cook a meal for your friends or family

tend to your plants

have a sabbath day to rest and delight

sleep in

go to the library

have a shower or bath by candlelight

say no to an event if you feel you should

watch the sunrise or sunset

have a solo tea party

meal plan

spend time on a project

have a picnic

spend time in the park

have a self care session

reflect on the past week and plan for the week ahead

slow monthly & yearly rhythms

Here are a few simple monthly and yearly rhythms to slow down. Some people may choose to do these monthly, quarterly, yearly or not at all. Choose what rhythms work for you!

visit friends and family who live afar

find ways to simplify the holiday season

take time to slow down and reflect on your birthday

evaluate your spending and align it with your values

go camping

go on a holiday

reflect on the past year

spring clean and declutter

have a digital detox

reflections for slowing down

What is my 'why' behind living a slower lifestyle?

What outcomes do I hope to foster from slowing down?

What slow activities or moments have I enjoyed in the past?

What habits could help me slow down and be present?

What are my values and could slowing down help support these values?

What areas of my life feel rushed?

How could slowing down help me to love people more?

my rhythms *to slow down*
What slow habits do you wish to implement in your life?

daily

weekly

monthly

_____
_____
_____
_____
_____
_____
_____
_____
_____

yearly

_____
_____
_____
_____
_____
_____
_____
_____
_____

slowing notes

habits

Whatever you have learned or received or heard from me, or seen in me—put it into practice. And the God of peace will be with you. — Philippians 4:9

Habits hugely shape our everyday lives. From the way we react in traffic to what we eat for breakfast, habits impact our emotions, relationships, faith and much more. And for many of us, we have a mixed bag of helpful and not so helpful habits. Gold star to those who floss!

If you're anything like me, creating a habit isn't always easy. However, there are three simple questions I find beneficial when choosing what habits to build into my life. The first one revolves around understanding my *why*—what is my motivation behind this habit? The second question is, does this habit truly align with my values? And lastly, does this habit honour the season of life that I'm currently in. Maybe for you, going to the gym five mornings a week works wonderfully, or perhaps you have young kids and this routine would cause stress and friction for you and your family.

The following pages present you with a few simple habits and rhythms that you may want to implement into your morning and evening rhythms. However, before implementing any of these, ask yourself: what is my 'why' behind this habit, does it align with my values and does it honour my season of life?

morning rhythm

The way we start our morning often spills into the rest of our day. Below is a list of simple habit ideas to implement into your morning to foster a slow, calm and joyful posture.

I encourage you to start simple and choose one or two to begin. You may want to add others later on!

get up at the same time each day

take a moment of gratitude upon waking

spend a couple of minutes in silence and solitude

spend time in prayer

spend a moment outside in the sun and fresh air

read a passage of scripture

take a walk outside	make a simple to-do list for the day	journal

make a gratitude list	read a book	do your skincare

drink a glass of water	do a light stretch or workout	enjoy a nutritious breakfast

incorporate deep breathing exercises	savour your first cup of tea or coffee	spend time on a hobby or creative project

evening rhythm

The way we choose to spend our evenings can directly impact the quality of our sleep and establish the tone for the following day. Below is a collation of habit ideas to incorporate into your nightly routine.

As I mentioned previously, feel free to start simply, choosing one or two to begin, and perhaps add others later on.

go to sleep at the same time every night

dim the lights around the house

prepare items and clothes for the next day

read a cosy book

limit screen time before bed

make a cup of herbal tea

listen to calming music	journal	unplug from work emails and to-dos
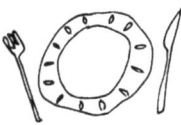		
avoid heavy meals close to sleeping	practice deep breathing exercises	reflect on positive moments from the day
	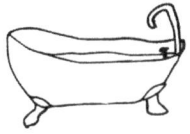	
do a light stretch	enjoy a warm bath or shower	pray before going to sleep

light a candle	do a relaxing skincare routine	tidy up the house

my habits & rhythms

Below offers you a space to bring awareness to the habits and rhythms that you want to build into your days. It also offers you the space to reflect on your why; your underlying motivation behind each habit.

habit	my *why*

habit	my *why*

habit notes

interruption

And we know that for those who love God all things work together for good, for those who are called according to his purpose. — Romans 8:28

The other day, I made myself a hot cup of earl grey tea (my current fav), grabbed my cosy white blanket and curled up on the couch ready to relax and unwind from the day. Splash! There went my beverage, spilt all over my not-so-white blanket and me. My mind quickly went to a whirlwind of annoyance at my clumsy self.

Life is full of interruptions and imperfections and when you have children, I imagine these increase tenfold. But if life is full of interruptions, it makes it even more valuable to enjoy the simple things as they occur: a baby's sweet smile, a kind word from a friend, a warm and hearty home cooked meal.

Our everydays are often full of surprises, unmet expectations and wonderful opportunities. And what we make of them can significantly impact our emotions, the people around us and our joy each day. I hope these next few pages inspire you to embrace the interruptions and imperfections of life and learn to see the good in them whenever you can.

navigating interruptions

Often the imperfection, interruptions and messiness of life can cause us to feel stressed, emotional or overwhelmed. Here are a few little reflections to help you grow and love others amidst those tricky moments.

Could there be a deeper reason why this interruption is having this response in me? Perhaps something else is already causing me stress?

Why is this interruption causing me to feel _____?

How can I use this interruption to help me grow in patience and love, despite things not going as planned?

How can I turn this interruption into something good?

Is there an expectation I have that is causing this interruption to feel harder?

Is there an expectation that I can let go of to make room for this interruption?

preparing for interruption

Although we cannot plan for every interruption, we can plan margin into our days. Additionally, we can make a habit of planning ahead. This can help us be more present and loving to those around us. Here are a couple of prompts to help you create margin and prepare for interruptions.

Are there any interruptions that I am regularly faced with and how can I plan better to be prepared for them? For example, do I get stuck in peak hour traffic often, which ends up making me late and frazzled? Instead, could I leave earlier or drive at a different time of day?

Do I often feel pulled in different directions and unable to focus? What boundaries can I set up so that I'm less distracted? Could I plan specific times for specific tasks so that I don't feel as overwhelmed?

Do I ever feel that I never have enough time? Is there anything in my life right now that isn't serving me or my family that I could stop/pause for this season of life?

planning ahead

Here are a few simple ideas to help you plan ahead to decrease stress when interruptions arise.

- create a simple to-do list the night before
- do weekly inventory checks (notice anything that needs to be re-purchased, repaired or removed)
- anticipate upcoming events and plan for them
- set up reminders for important deadlines or tasks
- allocate specific time blocks for tasks
- plan your outfit for the following day
- use a digital or physical planner
- schedule time to see loved ones
- meal prep your weekly staples
- plan for downtime and rest
- make a weekly meal plan
- create a simple budget
- use the slow cooker
- organise gifts early
- batch cook

my list of interruptions

This little list is a place for you to identify the areas in your life that you often feel interrupted in. As you take time to bring awareness to these situations, I invite you to also think and pray about how you can better equip yourself for them and learn to love others amidst the interruption.

interruption	reflection

interruption notes

gratitude

This is the day that the Lord has made; let us rejoice and be glad in it. — Psalm 118:24

I'll be the first to admit that I often forget to be grateful for all that I have. It's way too easy to get caught up in the never-ending cycle of wanting more, blaming others or worrying about what the next day will bring. However, this way of thinking can become a habit and soon enough it's the way we live; stressing, worrying and wanting.

I've heard it a thousand times—'just be grateful' or 'don't worry, it's not the end of the world.' I know people mean well, but often it's not that simple. Changing the way we think and interact with the world around us is a gradual transformation from within that requires intention, commitment and self-awareness. But it's well worth it!

Becoming a grateful person is not about blind positivity or ignoring the hard things in life, but rather about choosing to appreciate the good things in front of us no matter our circumstance. I adore this quote from the impressionist painter Camille Pissarro, who so eloquently said, 'Blessed are they who see beautiful things in humble places where other people see nothing.'

The next couple of pages share simple activities and ideas to help you create a posture of gratitude and thankfulness in your life. I hope these words open your eyes to see beautiful things in sometimes hidden places.

create a culture of *gratitude*

Creating a culture of gratitude around us isn't always natural. However, choosing to cultivate this in our relationships, families and environment is a beautiful way to help us focus on what is good and to lift others up along the way.

1. tell those you love how grateful you are for them
2. highlight what you're grateful for in conversations
3. thank people for the big and little things they do
4. give thank you gifts
5. ask others what they're grateful for
6. put up quotes, bible verses, photos that remind you to be grateful
7. send a message thanking someone for something they did for you

gratitude schedule

If you're looking to make gratitude a habit in your life, this little exercise may be helpful. Choose one or two of these daily rhythms to pair with gratitude every day.

1. upon waking
2. with your first cuppa
3. at breakfast
4. while brushing
5. during lunch
6. at dinner
7. before falling asleep

my gratitude schedule

This page is a place for you to write down a list of activities, habits or rhythms that you'd like to pair with gratitude each day.

when 	**gratitude prompt**

_____ 	_____
_____ 	_____
_____ 	_____
_____ 	_____
_____ 	_____
_____ 	_____
_____ 	_____
_____ 	_____
_____ 	_____
_____ 	_____
_____ 	_____
_____ 	_____
_____ 	_____
_____ 	_____
_____ 	_____

gratitude prompts

Here are a few simple questions to help you reflect on the goodness in your life.

What three things am I grateful for today?

Who am I grateful for today?

What around me in nature brings me joy?

What opportunities do I have that I'm thankful for?

In what ways have I grown recently?

What simple provisions or possessions do I have that I'm grateful for?

What small wins can I celebrate today?

What acts of kindness have I witnessed lately?

my gratitude list

Write down a list of things that you can be regularly grateful for. You may want to come back to this list whenever you're struggling to feel grateful.

_____

_____

_____

_____

_____

_____

_____

_____

_____

_____

gratitude notes

savouring

So I concluded there is nothing better than to be happy and enjoy ourselves as long as we can. And people should eat and drink and enjoy the fruits of their labour for these are gifts from God. — Ecclesiastes 3:12-13

The future can be a wondrous place. Full of endless possibilities and countless opportunities. I find myself there a lot. Thinking about what's to come, new projects and planning (lots of planning). And although being future minded does have its merits, it's also easy to brush past the now and forget to savour the present. However, when I choose to slow down and savour, I'm presented with a sense of calm, contentment and joy. Savouring the simple gifts of life, such as a warm shower, candy coloured sunset or a kind word from a friend, helps make life a sweeter and richer place.

This habit of savouring simple joys can be done through endless ways and continuously grown over time. The next couple of pages provide you with practical ways to incorporate the art of savouring into your life. We'll look at a little sequence of mind and body postures to help you motion through the act of savouring as well as a list of simple moments that you may wish to savour in your everyday life.

how to savour

1. pause

2. take a deep breath

3. bring yourself to the present

4. think about what is good about the moment

5. take a moment to soak up the goodness and be grateful

6. continue what you're doing with a fresh mindset

moments to savour in your *everyday*

your morning coffee

the clouds

a deep breath

smelling the flowers

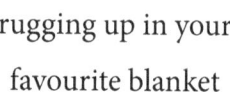

rugging up in your favourite blanket

a hot shower

stretching

a hot meal on a cold night

looking up at the stars

a stroll in your neighbourhood

a hug

a colourful sunrise

a hot cup of tea

snuggles with your pet

the first and last bite of a meal

taking your shoes off

chatting with a loved one

the stillness of the early morning

the smell of a book

when you notice a new leaf on your plant

lying down in bed after a long day

seeing rain droplets on leaves

a vibrant sunset

having a cold glass of water when you're thirsty

my list of things to savour

savour notes

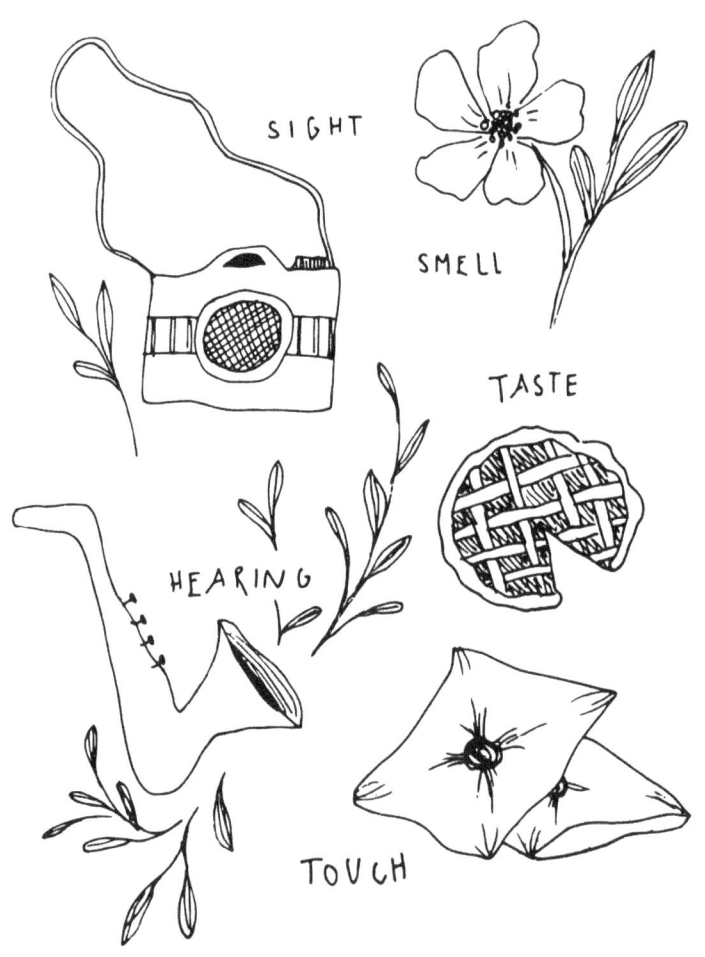

senses

Taste and see that the Lord is good; blessed is the one who takes refuge in him. — Psalm 34:8

We've been gifted with five incredible senses that help us engage with the world around us. Each sense is unique and opens countless opportunities to delight and witness God's goodness around us. Learning to engage more fully with our senses can help us become present and connected with our surroundings and those we love. It's easy to take our senses of sight, taste, touch, smell, and hearing for granted, however in these next few pages I invite you to become more present to them and grateful for the gift that they are.

Here is a simple exercise to help you connect with your senses. Right now, take a moment to notice 5 things you can see, 4 things you can feel, 3 things you can hear, 2 things you can smell and 1 thing you can taste.

As you go about your day, take time to slow down and sink into each of your senses. Let them delight you and surprise you by the goodness that they reveal. The next few pages offer reminders on the lovely everyday moments we can experience through our five senses.

what can you see?

cosy flickering candles

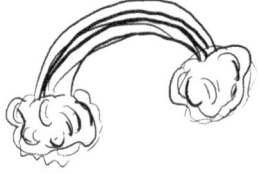

a colourful rainbow

the familiar face of a loved one

a well-loved bookshelf

a steaming cup of tea

fairy lights

handwritten notes

rain droplets

a starry night

flowers peeking through the pavement

lush green trees

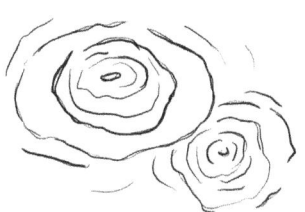

ripples in the water

soft warm hues filling the setting sky

what can you smell?

fresh herbs

burning candle

a campfire

hot coffee

freshly baked bread

clean laundry

wild flowers in the bush

salty ocean breeze

spiced chai tea

crisp autumn air

flowers in bloom

warm apple pie

freshly baked cookies

the rainy earth

perfume

what can you hear?

the swoosh of a turning page

laughter

a loved one on the phone

rustling leaves

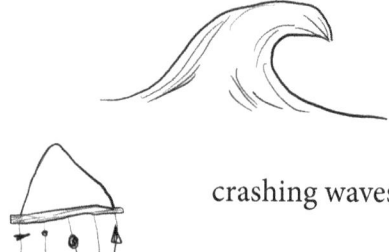

crashing waves

a crackling fire

gentle wind chimes

rain pattering on the roof

birds chirping out
the window

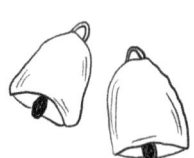

church bells

a sigh of contentment

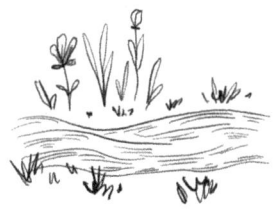

a babbling stream

soft acoustic guitar

a purring cat

what can you taste?

juicy citrus fruits

hot chocolate

warm homemade soup

zesty lemonade

piping hot muffins

sweet strawberries

cold watermelon

buttery popcorn

homemade berry jam

creamy ice cream

crisp sweet apples

soothing herbal tea

melt-in-your-mouth cheese

what can you feel?

the warmth of the sun

cosy jumper

curvy seashells

a baby's soft skin

fluffy pillows

brisk ocean breeze

fresh sheets

smooth flower petals

soft grass under your feet

falling rain

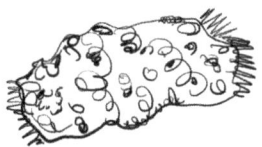

a snuggly blanket

puppy fur

smooth river stones

warm sand between your toes

senses notes

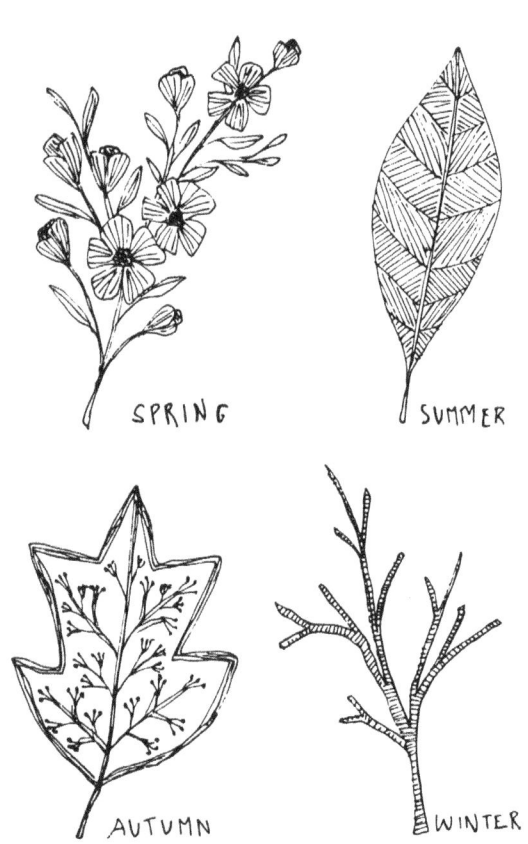

seasons

For everything there is a season, and a time for every matter under heaven: a time to be born, and a time to die; a time to plant, and a time to pluck up what is planted; a time to kill, and a time to heal; a time to break down, and a time to build up; a time to weep, and a time to laugh; a time to mourn, and a time to dance; a time to throw away stones, and a time to gather stones together; a time to embrace, and a time to refrain from embracing; a time to seek, and a time to lose; a time to keep, and a time to throw away; a time to tear, and a time to sew; a time to keep silence, and a time to speak; a time to love, and a time to hate; a time for war, and a time for peace. — Ecclesiastes 3:1-8

Each season in life and in nature's cycle, opens new opportunities to delight. Bringing a fresh perspective and experience of the world, learning to embrace the season that you're in is a beautiful way to stay grounded and connected with nature and those around you.

When I think of spring, the aroma of fresh flora and a plethora of fruits and veg comes to mind. Summer, I think of the longer days, evenings spent outdoors, and refreshing ocean swims. Autumn (my favourite!), I think of pulling out my cosy knits, always a hot tea in hand and a plethora of colourful leaves. Winter—snuggly blankets, coats, fluffy socks and the crisp ocean breeze. What comes to mind, when you think of each season?

One of my favourite ways to sink into each part of the year is to create a seasonal list of things to do. Over the page you'll see curated lists for each season to give you inspiration. However, I invite you to write down your own list of seasonal activities that inspire you to delight in each season!

spring *to-do list*

- [ ] try a new salad recipe
- [ ] buy a bunch of flowers
- [ ] go to your local markets
- [ ] read a book outside
- [ ] take a night stroll
- [ ] plan a weekend getaway
- [ ] simplify your closet
- [ ] go for a hike
- [ ] watch the sunrise
- [ ] make a smoothie
- [ ] make a seasonal fruit salad
- [ ] stroll around the park
- [ ] picnic outdoors
- [ ] plant colourful flowers
- [ ] listen to the birds chirping
- [ ] take a leisurely bike ride
- [ ] make a veggie patch
- [ ] wear light flowy clothes
- [ ] attend a spring festival
- [ ] lounge in a hammock
- [ ] stop to smell the flowers
- [ ] have a spring cleaning day
- [ ] start a herb garden

my spring *to-do list*

summer *to-do list*

- [ ] go out for ice cream
- [ ] swim in the ocean
- [ ] read by a pool
- [ ] have a BBQ picnic with friends
- [ ] snooze in a hammock
- [ ] watch the sunset
- [ ] have a beach bonfire
- [ ] go out stargazing
- [ ] watch a live event outdoors
- [ ] go on a road trip
- [ ] watch a movie at the drive in
- [ ] go camping by the water
- [ ] make fresh iced tea
- [ ] attend a night market
- [ ] eat cold watermelon
- [ ] visit an amusement park
- [ ] host a potluck dinner
- [ ] take a day trip
- [ ] try outdoor painting

my summer *to-do list*

autumn *to-do list*

- [ ] make your own chai latte
- [ ] find a cosy second hand knit
- [ ] bake an apple pie
- [ ] collect colourful leaves
- [ ] go camping in nature
- [ ] try a new soup recipe
- [ ] make a hot cocoa and cosy up
- [ ] go to the drive in with friends
- [ ] attend an autumn festival
- [ ] read by the fireplace
- [ ] try autumn photography
- [ ] wear a scarf and boots
- [ ] go to a book store cafe
- [ ] visit a farmers' market
- [ ] have a movie night with friends
- [ ] bake cinnamon scrolls
- [ ] explore a new town on foot

my autumn *to-do list*

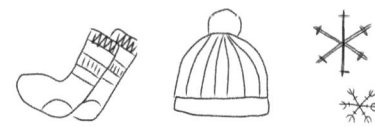

winter *to-do list*

- ☐ go ice skating
- ☐ wear fuzzy socks
- ☐ start a new cosy hobby
- ☐ bake cookies
- ☐ read by a fireplace
- ☐ knit a scarf
- ☐ visit a winter market
- ☐ make a comfort playlist
- ☐ play a winter sport
- ☐ make homemade soup
- ☐ wear a warm beanie
- ☐ make gooey hot brownies
- ☐ send handwritten cards
- ☐ listen to chilled jazz in the morning
- ☐ go on a long hike
- ☐ have a board games night
- ☐ host a potluck dinner party
- ☐ try a new winter recipe
- ☐ make a hot roast
- ☐ enjoy a candlelit dinner
- ☐ spend a night in a little cottage

my winter *to-do list*

seasons notes

outdoors

The heavens declare the glory of God; the skies proclaim the work of his hands. — Psalms 19:1

As a teenager, I had a somewhat intense love of picnics, fuelled by a close friend with a similar disposition. We picnicked copiously. We found such joy in collecting bits and bobs from the cupboard, baking sweet treats, and enjoying them beneath the warm sun and rustling leaves. What fond memories do you have of being out in nature? Learning to embrace the outdoors is a wildly rewarding way to find a deeper sense of calm and appreciation for the world we live in.

There are countless ways to embrace nature. One easy way to do this is to find activities that you already do and simply take them outside. Whether that's reading a book under a shady tree, drinking your morning coffee on the porch, taking your dinner to the beach, or painting in the park, with a little bit of imagination, there really are endless ways to enjoy the outdoors. The next few pages are filled with ideas, checklists and inspiration for embracing the natural world.

outdoor activity ideas

outdoor landscape art

collect leaves, rocks or seashells

fishing

play an outdoor sport

bird watching

camping

bike riding

snorkelling

swimming

have a campfire

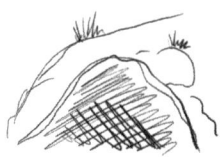

cave exploring

have a picnic

hiking

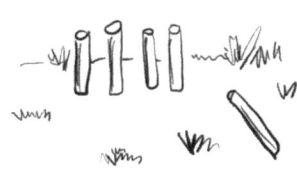

play lawn games

watch the sunrise

bush walking

how do you enjoy nature?

my outdoor activity ideas

what   where

beach day checklist

- ☐ towel
- ☐ sunscreen
- ☐ swimmers
- ☐ hat
- ☐ sunglasses
- ☐ beach umbrella
- ☐ sandals
- ☐ water bottle
- ☐ snacks
- ☐ beach bag
- ☐ picnic rug
- ☐ cooler
- ☐ beach chairs
- ☐ portable speaker
- ☐ book or magazine
- ☐ beach ball
- ☐ extra clothes
- ☐ inflatable floaties
- ☐ beach games

camping checklist

- [ ] tent
- [ ] sleeping bag
- [ ] torch
- [ ] matches
- [ ] pots & pans
- [ ] portable stove
- [ ] utensils
- [ ] clothes
- [ ] comfy shoes
- [ ] rope
- [ ] firewood
- [ ] water bottle
- [ ] sunscreen
- [ ] food
- [ ] foldable chairs
- [ ] toiletries
- [ ] garbage bags
- [ ] hat
- [ ] marshmallows
- [ ] portable charger
- [ ] camera
- [ ] books
- [ ] backpack
- [ ] mattress/mat
- [ ] first aid kit
- [ ] insect repellent

picnic planning

Picnics are a wonderful way to connect with nature, nurture relationships, slow down and enjoy some scrumptious food. What more could you want! Here is some inspiration to plan a wonderful picnic.

weather

Due to a picnic's outdoor nature, weather plays a significant role in the overall experience. Hence, here are a couple of weather considerations to ponder when planning your next picnic.

sunny weather

- location ideas: parks, beaches, lakes, hillsides, countryside, mountains, gardens
- notes: look for shady spots—perhaps a tree, beach umbrella or gazebo.

windy weather

- location ideas: parks, lakes, countryside, gardens
- notes: beaches and hills may be particularly windy, hence look for places that are less exposed to the elements.

rainy weather

- location ideas: under gazebos, undercover decks, car boot
- notes: rainy picnics can be such a fun way to bundle up and enjoy the outdoors despite the wet.

picnic checklist

Here's a little checklist of things you may want to bring on your next picnic, however you definitely don't need everything. Sometimes the best picnics are simple and spontaneous!

- [ ] picnic blanket
- [ ] sandwiches
- [ ] fruit
- [ ] snacks
- [ ] drinks
- [ ] sweets
- [ ] cooler
- [ ] cups
- [ ] plates
- [ ] napkins
- [ ] utensils
- [ ] cutting board
- [ ] knife
- [ ] cheese
- [ ] crackers
- [ ] condiments
- [ ] picnic basket

- [ ] sunscreen
- [ ] hat
- [ ] sunglasses
- [ ] insect repellent
- [ ] bin bag
- [ ] portable speaker
- [ ] lawn games
- [ ] pillows

outdoors notes

movement

"For while bodily training is of some value, godliness is of value in every way, as it holds promise for the present life and also for the life to come." — 1 Timothy 4:8

Recently I had a health circumstance that left me unable to walk without pain. Simple everyday activities became burdensome. Although I would not wish for this again, I loved the way it fostered a new humbled appreciation within me. No longer was a walk to the grocery store an inconvenience, but a joy. This time of immobility was a welcomed reminder of the gift that movement is. I've since noticed how the more I see moving my body as a gift, the more I enjoy it. The next few pages offer a variety of ways to move your body in a way that feels good to you. I hope these ideas inspire you to embrace an active lifestyle and propel a deeper appreciation for your body.

stretching poses

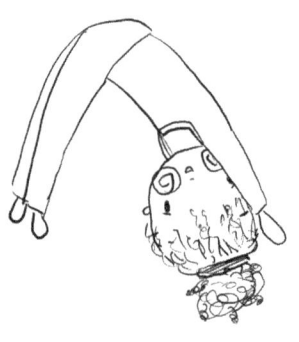

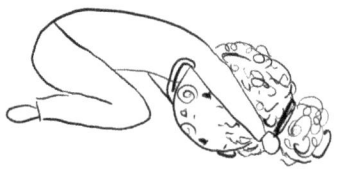

child's pose

downward dog

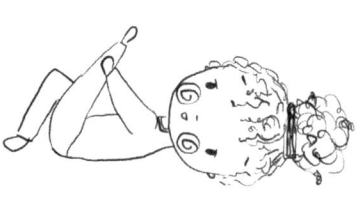

leg hold

butterfly

pike

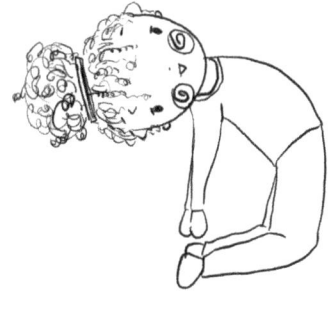
camel pose

straddle

upward dog

movement ideas

Here are a number of ideas for moving your body. Think about what would suit you, your family and lifestyle!

ice skating

skateboarding

karate

rock climbing

surfing

table tennis

snorkelling

running

dancing

 strength training

basketball

soccer

walking

hiking

everyday movement

Here are a couple of simple ways to add movement into your everyday living.

play with your pet

cooking and meal prep

stretch

dance in the kitchen

organise your home

walk in your lunch break

play with your children

movement notes

play

So I commend the enjoyment of life, because there is nothing better for a person under the sun than to eat and drink and be glad. Then joy will accompany them in their toil all the days of the life God has given them under the sun.
— Ecclesiastes 8:15

What does play mean to you? Often, I think of playing being a past time activity designed for children to enjoy. Yet if I stop to think, play is extremely present in my adult life. The *Oxford English Dictionary* defines play as 'to engage in activity for enjoyment and recreation rather than a serious or practical purpose.' Depending on your personality, life stage and circumstances, our day to day can often feel quite serious. Yes, life does call for us to be considerate, sincere and serious in many circumstances, however for many of us it can be easy to forget the joy of engaging in play. Through humour, games, hobbies, adventures and more, playing can help to foster connection with others, reduce unnecessary stress in our lives and open the door to creative pursuits. The next few pages are designed to remind you of the value of laughter and play and inspire you to implement moments of joy in your everyday.

indoor play

Here are a couple of ideas to spark inspiration for ways to play indoors.

play a card game

bake a treat

spend time on a hobby

share humorous stories

cosy up and read a novel

have a movie night

do a crossword or sudoku

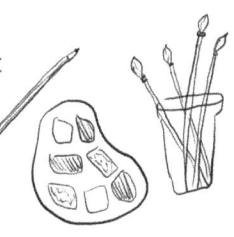

draw or paint

make a blanket fort

do a craft project

play a musical instrument

cook an old family recipe

host your friends

work on a puzzle

outdoor play

Here are a couple of ideas to enjoy the outdoors.

visit a local fair or festival

play a sport

go for a bike ride

go for a hike

garden

play catch with your pet

go for a swim

go bird watching

go rollerblading

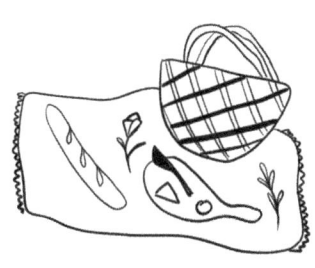
take a walk in the park

play miniature golf

have a picnic

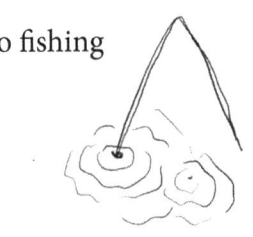
go fishing

go to an amusement park

play notes

creativity

And I have filled him with the Spirit of God, with wisdom, with understanding, with knowledge and with all kinds of skills—to make artistic designs for work in gold, silver and bronze, to cut and set stones, to work in wood, and to engage in all kinds of crafts. — Exodus 31:3-5

Do you see yourself as creative? Creativity comes in countless forms: writing, imagination, problem solving, humour, music—the list goes on. Whether you feel like you're a creative person or not, I believe we all have the inclination within us. Living creatively has been something I've valued for as long as I can remember. As a child I'd spend hours getting lost in creative pursuits—building extravagant blanket forts in the lounge room with my siblings (sorry mum), proudly crafting myself a paper outfit (yes shoes and hat included) or knitting a wonky scarf that looked more like an exotic hat. Without comparison, perfectionism, or time pressures, those early years often lead to unapologetic and flourishing creativity. However, as an adult the idea of being creative can at times feel irrelevant, overwhelming or unimportant.

I hope these next few pages, filled with simple hobby ideas and creative exercises, inspire you to ignite your creativity and find joy through your own unique expression!

handmade gift ideas

Here are 14 creative and meaningful DIY gift ideas to make for a loved one.

sewn item

knitted/crocheted item

baked treat

curated gift basket

handmade book

embroidered item

pottery

a story or poem

handmade card

bookmark

jewellery

candle

scrapbook/photo album

handmade artwork

a delicious meal

creative hobby ideas

craft
origami
scrapbooking
felt crafts
stencilling

art
painting
drawing
sketching
digital illustration
collage making
pottery
printmaking
mosaics
colouring in
interior design
sewing
soap making

digital
photography
videography
graphic design
digital animation

cosy
knitting
crocheting
embroidery
macramé
flower arranging

writing
calligraphy
short stories
poetry
write a book
fiction
hand lettering
blogging
bullet journaling

food
cake decorating
gourmet cooking
baking
chocolate making
bread making
food styling

music
song writing
playing an instrument
music producing
sound design
arranging music
singing

diy
upcycling preloved items
home projects
jewellery making
model building
candle making
tie-dyeing
woodworking

let's get creative!

The next couple of pages invite you to draw a couple of joyful illustrations. So grab your pencils and paper now! I'll wait...

teapot illustration

step 1

step 2

step 3

finished

tea cup illustration

step 1   step 2

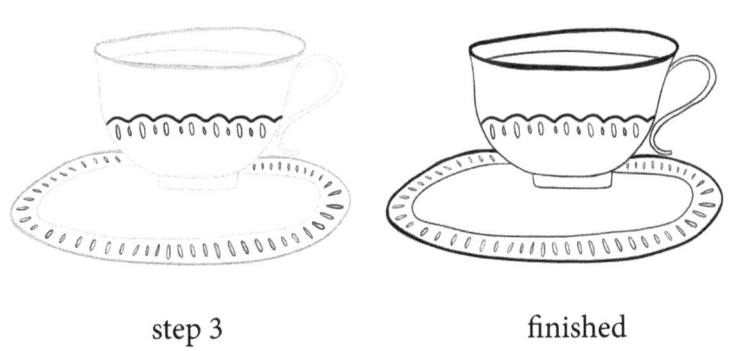

step 3   finished

house illustration

step 1

step 2

step 3

finished

flower bouquet illustration

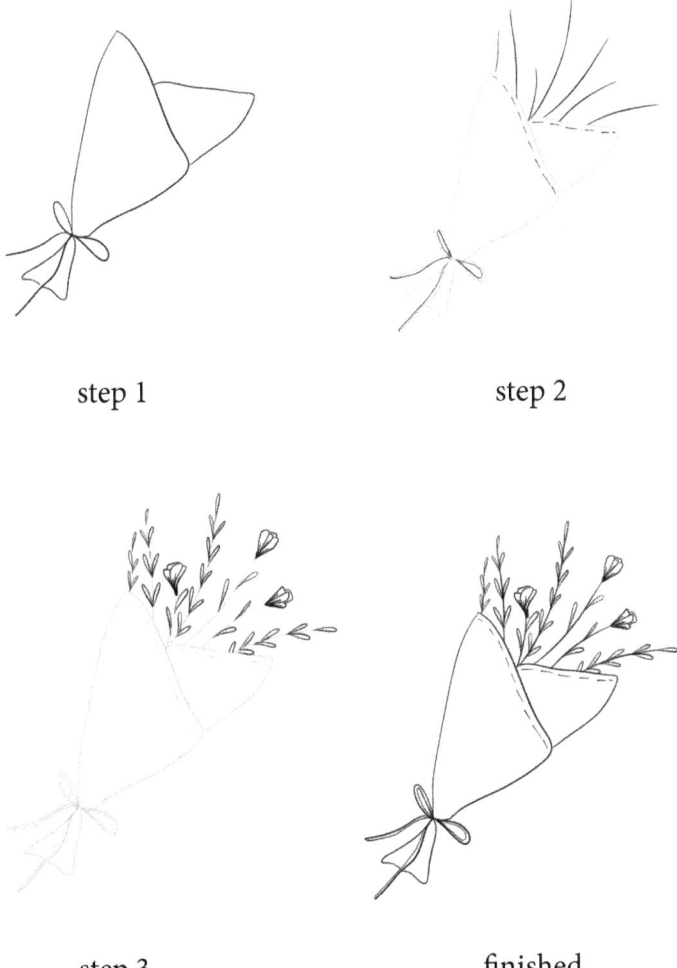

step 1

step 2

step 3

finished

creativity notes

order

For God is not a God of disorder but of peace—as in all the congregations of the Lord's people. — 1 Corinthians 14:33

Life is full of surprises, new adventures and sometimes messy situations. Have you ever noticed how when life feels chaotic, it's harder to feel at peace? You may experience a glimpse of this when you wake up to a kitchen bench stacked with dishes or when you're rushing out the door and can't find your keys.

Implementing a sense of order isn't about making your life structured and boring, but rather a tool for supporting a peaceful and intentional way of living. Simple acts such as making your bed or tidying the kitchen, may seem trivial, yet these small actions can help to create a peaceful environment that aids in reducing stress, increasing mental clarity and encouraging creativity and motivation.

For many of us, bringing order into our daily life can help support us and our families. Yet for others, we may already have a strong sense of order and the pursuit for perfection may be causing us stress or be linked to a need for control. Maybe you're living with multiple people or young children and having an ordered home and life is close to impossible. Hence, as you think about this topic, give yourself grace. Think about how order could serve you and your household in this season rather than be a burden or just 'another thing to do.'

intentional spaces

The way we design our spaces can hinder or help us. I love creating my environments to encourage order.

Here are a couple of questions to ask yourself as you design the spaces in your life to bring order, functionality and delight.

- Are there any areas in my home that collect clutter? If so, what can I change for this to work better?
- What objects in my everyday do I use the most, and how can I make these the most accessible?
- Are there any items that I hardly use and could be stored away, placed in a different spot or decluttered?
- Are there any habits in the home that are causing disorder?
- What habits within my home do I want to build to increase order?

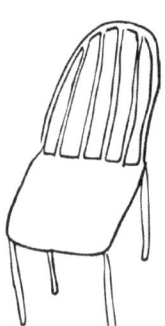

my household schedule

Here's a simple worksheet to help you plan and schedule your household tasks.

action	when	notes

order notes

simplicity

Then He said to them, 'Watch out! Be on your guard against all kinds of greed; life does not consist in an abundance of possessions.' — Luke 12:15

In 2023 my husband and I moved to a one bedroom apartment with minimal storage, a tight lounge room and modest kitchen. Yes, it was small, yet we saw this as an opportunity to cut down on clutter and simplify our life. We have loved the challenge of owning less and being intentional with what comes into our home, and plan to always make this a priority no matter the size of our future abodes. However, simplicity is not just about owning less, but about making time and space for the things that matter to you most.

I love how living simply reminds me to find joy in what I already have rather than constantly seeking something new or more exciting. It has helped me become more content in my circumstances and learn to be resourceful with what I have.

Simplifying your life can come in countless forms. Perhaps for you it's creating a simple budget, saying no to activities that don't serve your family or decluttering your home and living with less.

The next few pages are filled with ideas of how you can implement simplicity into your everyday and create room for a slow, intentional and joy-filled life.

ideas for simplifying

- make an easy system for taking reminder notes
- create a simple morning & evening rhythm
- make a list of easy nourishing go to meals
- unsubscribe from unnecessary emails
- give everything in your home a place
- wake up earlier than you need to
- declutter your items regularly
- make simple to-do lists
- make a simple budget
- say no to being busy
- do a digital declutter
- simplify your closet
- do one task at a time
- let go of perfection
- simplify your goals
- limit technology

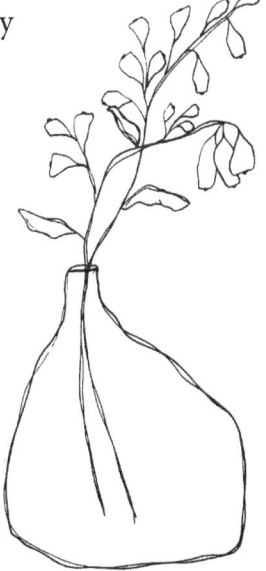

declutter checklist

Here's a list of household items for you to consider decluttering.

bedroom

- clothing
- shoes
- unused or broken furniture
- unused books
- extra bedding
- electronics and cables
- décor items
- extra hangers
- old jewellery
- unused electronics

bathroom

- old or expired toiletries
- empty products
- unused/expired makeup
- worn-out towels
- hair accessories
- old toothbrushes
- hair tools
- skincare products
- old soap dispensers
- unnecessary bath/shower products
- unused or broken razors

kitchen

- cleaning supplies
- pantry
- fridge
- freezer
- cupboards
- countertop
- tupperware
- cookware
- appliances
- tea towels
- junk drawer
- cookbooks

living room

- bookshelves
- coffee table
- entertainment unit
- décor pieces
- magazines
- pillows and blankets
- toys and games
- mounted shelving

questions to ask as you declutter

Is it broken, damaged or missing parts?

Do I own another item that serves the same purpose?

Am I hanging on to it out of guilt?

Have I used it much in the past year?

Do I really want to keep handling this item again?

Would I buy this again if I saw it today?

Is this item worth the space?

Is it worn out?

Is this piece in style?

Does it fit properly?

Do I truly love it?

simplicity notes

home

My people will live in peaceful dwelling places, in secure homes, in undisturbed places of rest. — Isaiah 32:18

For many of us, home is where we spend most of our time. Home offers a place to rest, recharge and offer hospitality to those around us.

Not long ago I found myself living in four different houses in the space of a couple of months. It was tiring. I'm sure many people can relate to just how exhausting moving can be. Growing up I had only lived in two houses and had never felt so uprooted in my life. This experience showed me how much having a regular place to rest and recharge is a true blessing and one that I don't want to take for granted.

Maybe you're moving from house to house, living abroad for the year, or in the house of your dreams. Depending on your circumstance, home can look wildly different for each person. However, there are many simple ways we can foster a more peaceful and beautiful space that brings joy to us and those we welcome in.

The next few pages offer ideas for designing your home purposefully and creating a beautiful atmosphere to encourage peace, rest and delight.

a peaceful home

Home is a safe haven, a place to rest, delight and welcome people in. The way we design our home environments impacts our lives immensely; both for our ability to recharge as well as thrive in our lives beyond the home.

There are endless ways to create a space that feels delightful, inviting and peaceful. From the lighting, colour choices and photos on display, each brings together the overall atmosphere. These choices can significantly influence our emotions, motivation and the way we spend our time. The next page offers ideas for creating a home that helps you and your household flourish.

atmosphere

How do you want your home to feel? This list below offers a variety of adjectives that could be used to describe your home. You may want to focus on a couple of them as you think about how to design your home environment.

- peaceful
- cosy
- warm
- bright
- colourful
- soft
- orderly

- luxurious
- earthy
- clean
- simple
- creative
- cheerful
- tranquil

- refreshing
- vibrant
- rustic
- homely
- welcoming
- lush
- spacious

tips for creating a peaceful home

- lighting: welcome bright lighting during the day (open blinds, curtains, windows) and create ambient lighting in the evening (candles, warm dimmed lights, fairy lights).
- style: create harmony around your home by finding a style that you love.
- simplicity: decrease clutter and simplify your home to foster a peaceful environment.
- zones: create specific areas in your home for certain activities to increase focus and motivation for each activity.
- organisation: give everything in your home a place and create systems to foster flow and order in your home.
- nature: bring natural elements into your home to give life and beauty to your space.
- senses: consider each of the five senses as you design your home—what can you hear, smell, touch, taste and see?
- personal touch: each home is a personal reflection of you and your household. Adding unique items such as photos, artworks and sentimental keepsakes can help to foster a joyful and homely atmosphere.

home notes

nourish

"I give you every seed-bearing plant on the face of the whole earth and every tree that has fruit with seed in it. They will be yours for food." — Genesis 1:29

Have you ever picked up a bright rosy ripe strawberry; taken a slow bite as the sweet tangy flavour implodes in your mouth, giving you a pure moment of delight? I have. Although far too often I'm simply in a rush, multitasking or too distracted to truly enjoy the nourishing goodness in front of me. However, when I choose to be slow and mindful, I've found there to be so much joy in savouring each bite.

I'm so grateful for the way God has made such a beautiful array of colourful, flavourful and delicious foods designed for us to enjoy and be nourished by. However, in this day and age, it's easy to lose connection with the way our food has been sown, grown and transported to our table. I too have been guilty of taking the very substance that keeps me alive for granted. However, it's humbling to appreciate what has been laboured over for a simple meal to reach our plate.

I hope these next few pages inspire you to find a deeper gratitude for all the wonderful foods we have been gifted and to ignite a greater passion for nourishing yourself joyfully.

mindful eating

Here are 5 simple mindful eating habits that you may wish to build into your daily life.

1. Pause and say a prayer of gratitude before your meal.

2. Sit down while eating.

3. Take a moment to appreciate all that has happened

   for the food to reach your plate.

4. Take a deep breath before a meal.

5. Eat slowly and savour each bite.

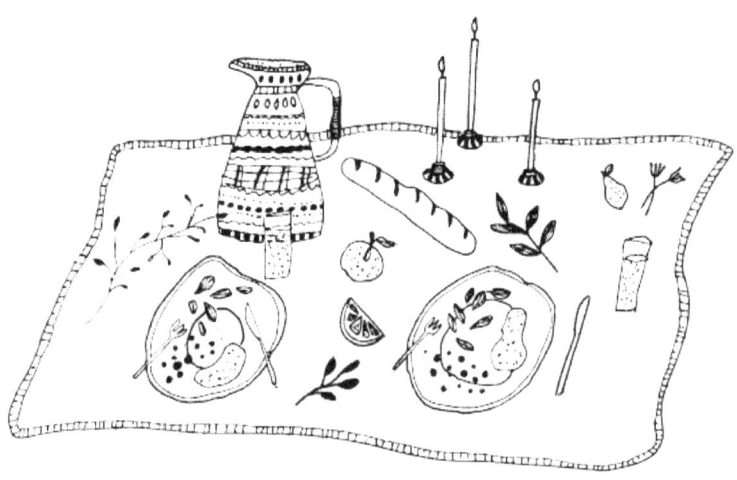

the story of an apple pie

Thinking about where our food comes from and all that has happened for it to be on our table is humbling. What a blessing farmers are! This little simplified poem is a reminder of the time and effort that goes into a simple baked good.

The seeds are sown in the soil

Then the seeds begin to sprout

A strong tree grows amidst the toil

Then apples are plentiful about

They're chopped, peeled and prepared for a boil

Then hot pie is served that is scrumptious no doubt

nourish notes

work

Whatever you do, work heartily, as for the Lord and not for men. — Colossians 3:2

The *English Oxford Dictionary* defines work as an 'activity involving mental or physical effort done in order to achieve a purpose or result.' Yes work may look like a 9 to 5 job. However for many of us our work isn't so straight forward. Maybe your work looks like caring for your family and household or serving your community or church or perhaps studying late each night for your final exams.

I believe that we are all stewards of God's beautiful earth and were created to work in a way that aligns to God's vision for human flourishing. And although I'm far from perfect, I've found there to be such a lightness and joy when I choose to glorify God through my work rather than striving to fill my own desires.

Work will play a different role in many of our lives and will likely change throughout different seasons. And although the challenges, beauty and value of our work is deeply individual, for many of us there are countless opportunities to invite joy in amidst it all.

I hope the next few pages fill you with inspiration to seek out the good, find ways of loving others richly and glorify God wherever your work may take you.

reflections on work

Here are a couple of scripture verses to reflect on as you think about your work.

Commit to the Lord whatever you do, and he will establish your plans. — Proverbs 16:3

Anyone who has been stealing must steal no longer, but must work, doing something useful with their own hands, that they may have something to share.
— Ephesians 4:28

The Lord God took the man and put him in the Garden of Eden to work it and take care of it. — Genesis 2:15

So whether you eat or drink or whatever you do, do it all for the glory of God. — 1 Corinthians 10:31

In the same way, let your light shine before others, that they may see your good deeds and glorify your Father in heaven. — Matthew 5:16

my reflections on work

How can I use my work to bless others?

_____

How can I love others well through my work?

_____

What skills do I have that I could use for good?

_____

Do I feel as though my plans are committed to the Lord?

_____

What is my motivation behind my work? Am I working for others or God?

_____

Do my values align with the way I'm working?

_____

What simple joys do I experience in my work?

_____

_____

_____

work notes

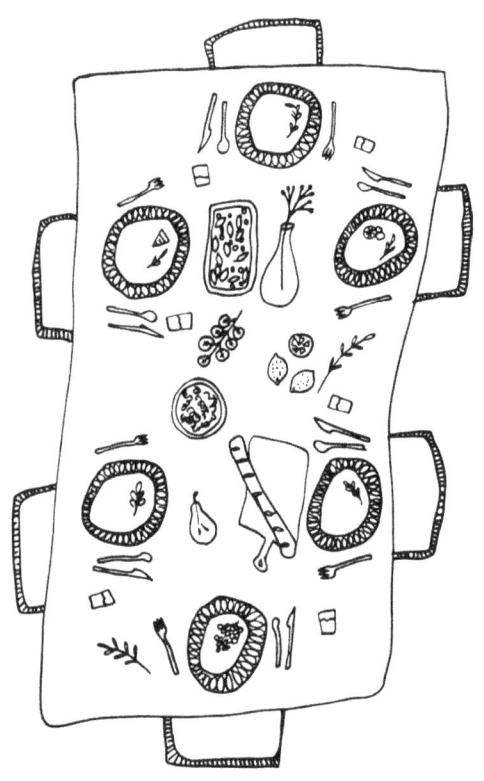

gather

Above all, love each other deeply, because love covers over a multitude of sins. Offer hospitality to one another without grumbling. Each of you should use whatever gift you have received to serve others, as faithful stewards of God's grace in its various forms. — 1 Peter 4:8-11

The older I get the more I realise the importance of community and investing in relationships. It's easy to get caught up in the fullness of life, endless to-dos or just simply opt for a restful night in (which has its time and place). Investing in people takes time and commitment yet is well worth the effort. I like to think of my community in three parts: 1. those in my outer circle (the broader community such as the barista across the street); 2. those in my inner circle (people who I see regularly such as work colleagues); and 3. those who are my circle (these could include your spouse, close friends, and family). Each type of relationship offers unique opportunities for meaningful connection.

Over the next few pages there are numerous ideas for how we can foster rich relationships with those around us and love those in our community well.

hospitality

So many of my most precious memories are from being around people sharing a meal—sharing our lives.

For many of us hospitality comes easy. Good food, people we love, and possibly even dessert (count me in!). Yet for others it may cause stress, overwhelming feelings, or simply feel like a waste of time. However, as I read the scriptures, I'm reminded and encouraged by God's heart toward hospitality and having a servant heart toward those in our community. Hospitality offers us a beautiful doorway to building meaningful relationships and a powerful opportunity to care for and love people well.

I encourage you to find simple ways, that honour your season of life, to welcome people into your home and heart.

Share with the Lord's people who are in need. Practice hospitality. Bless those who persecute you; bless and do not curse. Rejoice with those who rejoice; mourn with those who mourn. Live in harmony with one another. Do not be proud, but be willing to associate with people of low position.
— Romans 12:13-16

ways to build community

build a relationship
with your neighbours

volunteer at a local
organisation

join a sports team

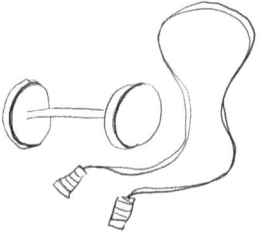

make friends at
your gym

attend local events

engage in conversation with
people around you

join a book club

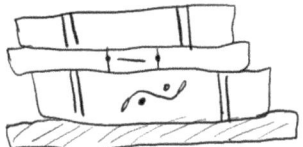

start your own club

get to know your colleagues

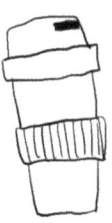

make friends at your local coffee shop

get involved in a church community

join your local park run

event ideas

Hosting an event is such a beautiful and intentional way to bring people together! Birthdays and milestones offer the perfect opportunity to plan a wonderful event, however you don't just have to use these life events to host something memorable and exciting. Have you ever hosted a themed event for your family or friends for no particular reason? Here's your permission slip! I hope these ideas below offer a spark of inspiration to bring together your community to enjoy a joyful event.

- DIY workshop
- popcorn and movie night
- book swap and discussion
- outdoor movie screening

- stargazing by the beach
- cosy board game night
- group workout class
- campfire and smores
- afternoon tea party
- pottery workshop
- spa day at home
- outdoor brunch
- potluck dinner
- dessert party
- paint and sip

celebration

I'm a big believer in celebrating the little things, as well as the grand, life changing moments too. There is such delight found in taking the time to gather, be present and celebrate wholeheartedly with those you love. Here are a couple of ideas for things we can celebrate as well as some ideas on how to celebrate them!

things to celebrate

- achieving a goal
- completing your to-do list for the day
- birthdays
- newborn baby
- learning something new
- good news
- weddings
- a new job
- small wins that you're proud of
- cleaning your house
- exercising
- finishing a project
- going to the dentist!
- seeing friends and family

ways to celebrate

- watch the sunset
- enjoy your favourite beverage
- gather your friends and family for a meal
- take a day off
- make your favourite meal
- have a piece of cake!
- spend time with those you love
- watch a movie
- take a bath
- do a little self-care
- take a holiday
- spend time in nature

meaningful conversation

Here are some conversation starters to ignite delightful and meaningful connection.

- What and who inspires you?
- Is there a book or movie that changed your life?
- Describe your perfect day.
- If you could meet anyone, living or dead, who would it be?
- What do you value most in a friendship?
- Do you have a skill or hobby you'd love to learn?
- Your favourite travel destination and why?
- A cause or charity you're passionate about?
- If you had a time machine, where and when would you go?
- What's a challenging experience that shaped you?
- How do you practice self-care?
- A memorable lesson you've learned recently?
- Your go-to way to relax and unwind?
- A goal or dream you're currently working towards?

- Describe a moment that made you laugh uncontrollably.
- What's a small gesture that makes your day better?
- A quote or mantra that resonates with you?
- If you could have dinner with anyone, who would it be?
- A piece of advice you'd give to your younger self?
- What do you appreciate most about your life right now?

gather notes

giving

Command those who are rich in this present world not to be arrogant nor to put their hope in wealth, which is so uncertain, but to put their hope in God, who richly provides us with everything for our enjoyment. Command them to do good, to be rich in good deeds, and to be generous and willing to share. — 1 Timothy 6:17-18

Have you ever noticed how giving is often much more fulfilling than receiving? The purpose of this little book has been to draw our attention to the abundant gifts that we have in our lives and to learn to slow down, savour, and receive these gifts with gratitude. However, a rich life is not just about holding tight to the gifts we have, but rather holding them with an open hand, as we look out for how we can share our blessings with those around us.

> John answered, "Anyone who has two shirts should share with the one who has none, and anyone who has food should do the same."
> — Luke 3:10-11

I believe that the greatest gift of all is one that is meant to be shared with every single person. Jesus, the Son of God lived a sinless life of humility, compassion, love and devotion to his Heavenly Father. He then made the greatest sacrifice one can make, his life. He died an undeserved, horrible, painful death as atonement for our sinfulness, so that you and I may be completely forgiven and have our relationship with our Heavenly Father restored.

Jesus offers us a remarkable example of sacrifice, and through his life and teachings, invites us to live selfless lives too. Matthew 20:28 beautifully reveals to us Jesus' heart and purpose—'just as the Son of Man did not come to be served, but to serve, and to give his life as a ransom for many.'

So, as you contemplate all the beautiful gifts of this world and seek to share with those around you, my prayer is that you would live the everyday holding the greatest gift of all close to your heart.

giving to your community

"Not all of us can do great things. But we can do small things with great love." — Mother Teresa

Here are a few little ways that we can practice generosity in our everyday lives.

- share useful information with others
- assist people carrying heavy loads
- offer your seat on public transport
- pay for a stranger's meal
- support a local business
- compliment a stranger
- be courteous in traffic
- leave a generous tip
- smile at a stranger
- donate to a charity
- hold the elevator

giving to your loved ones

Here are a couple of ideas to show generosity toward your loved ones.

- cook or bake something special
- offer words of encouragement
- be reliable and dependable
- organise a fun outing
- initiate a video call
- lend a listening ear
- plan a thoughtful surprise
- share a heartfelt compliment
- express your gratitude for them
- help with a task or project
- be there in times of need
- send a handwritten note
- surprise them with a gift
- celebrate their achievements
- forgive and let go of grudges
- celebrate their special occasions
- support their goals and dreams

my gift to you

download your free workbook

I have created a *Love the Everyday Workbook* to help you make actionable steps towards a joyful life. Head to my website (humblydesigned.com/workbookgift) to download your free gift!

giving notes

share your joys!

Listening to what other people are delighting in amongst their day to day is a joy in itself. I'd love for you to come say hi and join the conversation over on Instagram (@humblydesigned) and share what your everyday joys are!

acknowledgements

I want to say a huge thank you to my mum for all the time, effort and encouragement she's given. I love you! I also want to thank my incredible editor Amanda, it's been an absolute joy to work with you. Lastly, thank you to my wonderful husband, family and friends who have made my ordinary life so rich and beautiful. You know who you are.

www.ingramcontent.com/pod-product-compliance
Lightning Source LLC
Chambersburg PA
CBHW052113200426
43209CB00057B/1602